The
Violet Flame:

A Game Changer!

The

Violet Flame:

A Game Changer!

Transform your life with 15 minutes of daily decreeing & create true abundance.

by

Denise Kane

ISBN: 978-0-578-44103-0

Visit me at
www.denisekane.com
for workshops, news and events.

Violet Star Press

Dedication

I'm honored and grateful to share these lovingly created decrees with you and the world. I trust they will empower you to embrace this powerful tool, to live your true authentic self, and claim freedom too.

Contents

My story . . .   9

What is the Violet Flame?   15

How does the Violet Flame work & how to use it?   19

How to create the life of your dreams with the Violet Flame?   25

Violet Flame Decrees . . .   30

Violet Star Angel Decrees   60

Super 7 Crystal Message   63

One-Liners   64

Declaration of Independence   66

Violet Pictures   68

Parting Words   69

Acknowledgments   70

About the Author   71

My story . . .

To say the violet flame consumed my life in 2011 is an understatement. I discovered the violet flame at an event that spring. The captivating speaker was Patricia Cota-Robles. When the talk finished, I purchased her book *The Violet Flame: God's Gift to Humanity,* even though my mind said, *Why do I need this?* I kept hearing another voice say, "Buy it!" So I did, and I'm euphoric I listened to my intuition. In the days that followed, I eagerly read through her book, learning about the violet flame and how to use it. Patricia's book contains many decrees (affirmations, prayers, invocations), for all situations . . . physical healing, forgiveness, financial freedom, peace, etc. I began decreeing daily, and before long I felt a shift in my consciousness. This shift—*transformation*— made me feel lighter, happier. And it freed me from (*some*) of the stresses of daily life. Everything flowed with greater ease and enjoyment. I continue to invoke the violet flame to this day, and I'll explain later how the wonders of this gift grace my life.

One day, about six months into decreeing, a thought surfaced of a past annoying work situation. To my surprise, when I recalled this thought, it was no longer irritating—but transformed. I actually laughed out loud and thought, *What happened?* I scratched my head in disbelief; realizing I'd just experienced a life lesson, part of my personality's growth. I know in my heart I have the violet flame to thank for this miraculous change of awareness. Since then, many such beliefs and experiences have gone through this astonishing metamorphosis. Old nagging memories, feelings, thought patterns and fears diminished or dissolved, the sting taken out. So liberating!

Fast forward three years . . . I received guidance one morning during meditation to teach the violet flame in a workshop. This was new for me. I worked in corporate for thirty-eight years but never had the opportunity to develop a Microsoft PowerPoint presentation or teach classes. After considerable research, I devised the concept and learned how to work with PowerPoint (thanks to the kind professor on YouTube). It was a year or more in the incubator before going live. I must say, this was way out of my comfort zone. Fear welled up inside me, but I felt bound to share this immense gift with humanity. There was no turning back—I just *knew* I had to muster up the courage. Witnessing my dramatic changes with the violet flame first-hand propelled me to rise above those scary emotions; from personal experience I was convinced this critical knowledge would benefit people on multiple levels, and help them embrace peace, well-being and happiness—for starters!

The first workshop was at my home in November of 2015 to test the waters—with eleven participants. The two-hour class went well. One thing I'll never forget was the feeling after—something I'd never before felt. Exhilaration, amazement and deep stillness, all rolled into one, radiated through my entire body. I couldn't wait for the next class.

Now, eleven workshops later, each one has taken me on a journey of expansion, growth and healing. Jaw-dropping events have transpired—for the participants as well. Burdens have been released on the spot with witnesses to affirm the magnitude of this extraordinary gift. One gentleman who attended with his wife experienced a tremendous weight lifted from his shoulders. He was carrying lots of resentment and unforgiveness over a family issue. As the class was reciting a decree together, he yelped and started crying. This in turn made his wife and the participants well up too—a very emotional experience. He said he finally felt a peace he hadn't felt since his wedding day, twenty years ago. He shared with me recently that using the violet flame daily has deepened the peaceful feeling, and the old memories that used to annoy him no longer do: they've lost their emotional charge. Better yet, he's been able to meet in person those involved in his family issues and forgive.

For another participant, the sadness and guilt over putting her dog to sleep was overwhelming. She thought she'd never feel good again and was amazed at how easily and effectively the violet flame healed her pain.

There are way too many poignant events to rehash here; however, one of the most momentous was when at the end of class a lady was weeping. I asked if she wanted to share; she said that morning she was contemplating suicide but had meditated and heard the guidance to go to Dancing Moon (bookstore where the event was held) and find the *flame*. So she pulled herself together, even though she was skeptical. Arriving at the bookstore, she wandered around, not sure exactly what she was looking for. Suddenly she saw the flyer and checked her watch; the workshop was starting *in two minutes*. She realizes to this day it was divine timing and her angels' help that saved her life.

An unexpected event happened after the first workshop. A few participants wanted to practice the tools and techniques, so I suggested we meet at my home. Amazingly enough, we've been meeting every Sunday since, for over three years. We've created a Lightworkers' group and named ourselves the *Violet Stars*. Our mission is to raise personal and collective consciousness. St. Germain, the Ascended Master and Guardian of the Violet Flame, oversees these gatherings. He provides a timely message weekly and occasionally, a powerful guided healing meditation. I began channeling St. Germain live with an audience in August 2017. Channeling is giving voice to the Light. These weekly messages may be found on my YouTube channel.

When I was preparing to teach the first workshop, I was inspired to created two decrees. I realized these would be powerful devices for the participants to recite out loud together, and as the above stories demonstrate, they were. Soon after, my creative juices started flowing, and I had the urge to create more, and more, and more, until one day I realized there were forty-six decrees: for empowerment; grief; forgiveness; healing physically, mentally and emotionally; balancing and cleansing the chakras; self-love; soul's purpose; Divine government; abundance; anger; mind chatter; healing the Earth and more. This book will provide you with the tools needed to transform your life, by demonstrating how to transmute the unwanted and replace it with whatever it is you desire.

To this day, I am a devotee of the flame, reciting decrees daily for specific issues in my life, to obliterate worldwide problems and to conceive a healthy beautiful planet. The violet flame will enrich your life in ways you cannot imagine. And best of all, it's easy to use.

What is the Violet Flame?

The violet flame is one of the most powerful spiritual gifts ever given to the people on Earth. It's a combination of the blue flame of Divine Father—God's Will and Power—and the pink flame of Divine Mother—Divine Love. When you invoke the violet flame—with a decree (prayer)—these two flames coalesce in your heart and create the color violet; hence, the violet flame. St. Germain is the Ascended Master of the Seventh Ray, guardian of the violet flame and Chohan to usher in the Age of Aquarius and shift to higher consciousness. The Seventh Ray holds the Divine qualities of freedom, forgiveness, mercy, compassion, transmutation and God's infinite perfection. An Ascended Master is a very evolved being, who has walked the Earth, like Jesus and Buddha. Since he has walked in our shoes, he understands the challenges of daily human life. You are welcome to call upon him for assistance.

St. Germain requested the violet flame from God to help humanity, and after a Divine dispensation it was brought to the planet during the early twentieth century. It was bestowed to a few people living a higher-consciousness life, who would value this gift wisely. Once the Divine saw that the people on Earth would embrace the flame, it was shared. According to Patricia Cota-Robles, whom I have great confidence in and have worked with extensively, "In 1936, St. Germain began revealing information about the violet flame to awakening Humanity. At that time, even the Lightworkers were able to withstand only the gentlest frequencies of this Sacred Fire. St. Germain started by teaching Lightworkers how to use the violet flame's gentle qualities of mercy, compassion and forgiveness. As time progressed, Lightworkers learned to use the frequencies of transmutation and purification. Eventually the violet flame frequencies of justice, liberty, freedom, opportunity and victory became known to us."

Very few knew about the violet flame and its capabilities until recently. If humanity could fathom the incredible transformative power it contains, many more would be avidly participating with daily invocation.

The violet flame works each and every time it is invoked (reciting a decree or affirmation) at an atomic level, by transmuting negative energy into positive. I was spellbound when I tried to comprehend the magnitude of this statement. It's like a super-duper cleaning product that goes deep down to the cellular level and osculates—like a washing machine—removing the dirt and grime, including pain and negativity. It's not necessary for you to understand, or even believe, at the outset, to get results: the violet flame will do its deep cleansing and healing. Plain and simple, it works scientifically, each and every time; on whatever it is you wish to transmute, whether from your physical, emotional and mental bodies, your home, office, food, water or anywhere else on the planet. Perhaps you wish to release those useless burdens, thought patterns—victim consciousness, judgment, criticism—and obsolete beliefs, as well as baggage you've been carrying for lifetimes. Best of all, it gets to the root of the matter, so you won't be weighed down any longer. It's even handy in resolving relationship issues by transmuting blockages on the cords between us and others. It also releases any blockages held from the past or even the thought patterns and beliefs that were given at birth from our family's DNA. There are 101 uses for the violet flame, and I'm sure you'll discover more. Another wonderful daily use is to place a cosmic filter of violet light between you and the computer, television and phone (decree located in *One-Liners* section). This protects you from negative and discordant energy that may radiate from these devices, including another's negativity.

The violet flame will also transmute forgiveness issues, fear, pain, negativity, anger, blame, stress, grief, guilt, anxiety and anything else under the sun. St. Germain wishes you to know that whatever you are suffering or in pain from, it can and will be alleviated with daily devotion. He recommends decreeing a minimum of fifteen minutes a day for maximum benefit, and encourages you to do a thirty-day challenge—the more effort, the greater and quicker the results. You've got nothing to lose but fifteen minutes. As you memorize decrees, you'll be able to repeat them in traffic jams, while walking the dog, washing dishes and during other mundane times of the day your mind is idle. Any decreeing is better than none. And always say them with reverence, focus and intention.

How does the Violet Flame work & how to use it?

The violet flame is activated—*turned on*—by invocation; it's called forth with a decree, or affirmation, and begins working *immediately* on healing your body, transmuting negativity, alleviating anger and dissipating fear or any other emotion that is resonating at a lower frequency/vibration in your physical and energy body/field. Sometimes, however, the results are not yet discernable until this spiritual energy saturates your energy field. Even though you may not see through your physical senses that anything is changing, *it is*. When the violet flame is invoked, it travels down your hara line (see below) from the heart of God into your heart, to be directed where it is needed. Your hara line is a straight crystalline line of light extending from the Sacred Heart of God, through your being at the deepest level, into the crystalline core of Mother Earth. Decrees and affirmations give the mind a tool to focus on a specific intention and to direct the violet flame to a desired area. When you recite decrees, there is a buildup of spiritual energy in your aura. As you daily decree, this energy becomes an indomitable force to provide protection for your entire being on all levels—physical, mental and emotional—keeping illness, others' emotional residue, destructive thought forms at bay.

After two years of daily decreeing, while I was on a spiritual trip the violet light showed up on a picture in my camera. I eagerly took it to my traveling companion, thinking it would quickly disappear. Well, it didn't, and since that time there have been many instances the violet light has made itself known. The reason for this occurring was a saturation of the violet flame in my aura. It's thrilling to get tangible proof that this spiritual stuff is real.

Here's the physics behind how the violet flame works. When invoked—*called forth*— it changes the vibration of an atom. Everything in the Universe is energy. As Albert Einstein put it so succinctly, "Energy cannot be created or destroyed, it can only be changed from one form to another." Hence, when the violet flame is invoked, it transforms negative energy into positive and gives us the power to heal and be free of that burden. Negative energy can become stuck in the atoms in our bodies. When this happens, the electrons oscillate around the atom at a slower rate and your body vibrates at a low vibration. When the violet flame is invoked, it transforms—*since energy cannot be destroyed*—this negative energy into Light, which enables the electrons to oscillate faster, raising your vibration. When you have a higher vibration, there is more spiritual energy—Light—in your body, which restores well-being, energy, vitality and exhilaration.

However, for the manifestation to occur in the physical, there must be—during the healing process—sufficient spiritual energy in your body and energy field. There are many layers involved with healing, like peeling an onion. Our personal journey and evolution bring tests. Many times we resist learning the lesson and hinder our progress. Our pain is an indication of a thought or feeling that is stuck in our energy field and manifests in the physical body. When we're able to make a change in our thoughts, by removing those that are not empowering and positive, and use the violet flame to transmute dense energy from our energy body (aura), we will see radical changes to the way we feel, both physically and emotionally. To take responsibility for our thoughts, words, actions and feelings is a crucial step in our development. When we waver, the violet flame is there for us, to transmute negativity into positivity.

When I began using the violet flame, I was working for a major airline, on the ground at the airport. Can you imagine the detrimental energies that permeated the terminal? Before I left home for work, I'd say a decree (see *One-Liners* section) and imagine the terminal engulfed with the violet flame. During my shift I would reaffirm and *see* the flame saturating the space. I noticed a difference in the passengers, other employees and myself. At this time, my position was Manager on Duty. What was astonishing was the employees realized that when I was on duty the day flowed, it was peaceful, every-thing ran smoother, and people were nicer, even if we were having an off-schedule operation (due to weather, mechanical problems, etc.). They felt as-sured, since I was on duty, it would be okay. By all means, I am not tooting my own horn. When vari-ous employees from different work groups would tell me this on practically a daily basis (and they still tell me to this day even though I'm retired), I took notice. What better way to demonstrate the effectiveness of the flame but at an airport.

You can use the violet flame anytime, not just during meditation. It's extremely beneficial to start the day decreeing—to achieve a high, good-feeling vibration—and then set intentions. It's best to say decrees in multiples of three. In so doing, you align your conscious mind with your higher self and your Divine Self (I AM Presence). Your I AM Presence is your Divine Self, you as God created. When you say, "I AM," you connect to this expansive aspect of yourself and God, thus bringing into your reality what you invoke. Become mindful of what is enhan-cing your life and what is not and make the switch. These two words can—and will—change your life.

A way to rev up the decree is to say it aloud. When I first started, I was decreeing silently, until one day I vocalized and it almost blew my socks off. When possible, speak them, but know they are working regardless. Another wonderful facet of decreeing is visualizing. Seeing in your mind's eye —imagination—an image of what you are saying will greatly enhance the decree. Visualizing gives the mind a mental picture. It also helps our unconsciousness mind accept this as our reality, and soon enough, it will manifest. For example, as you say a decree for healing, visualize the violet flame engulfing your physical body and direct the flame to a specific body part. See the violet flame oscillating, transmuting the pain and bringing in relief, comfort, flexibility and relaxation. Or maybe you wish to transmute a fear-based thought. Again, as you say the decree, visualize the powerful force transmuting the thought and bringing in Light. One more thing to amp up your decrees is to focus on your breathing. As you breathe intentionally and become aware, your breath will naturally slow; you'll be more relaxed and meditative—bringing your focus in, instead of on the outer world. There are many breathing techniques available on YouTube and the internet, as well as fascinating Ted Talks on the topic.

It's not necessary for you to use all of these decrees on a daily basis. Discover those that you enjoy and find appealing. This may shift as your life evolves and your experiences unfold. Share them with friends and family and decree together in prayer circle groups. You may even wish to create some decrees of your own. Most of all, have fun and know you are impacting the world in far-reaching ways.

There's a decree called the "Declaration of Independence," which is the oath for the Violet Stars Lightworkers Group. This powerful proclamation holds intense energy. I received guidance to create this six months after forming the Violet Stars. Unable to think of a title I asked St. Germain, who eagerly stated, "the Declaration of Independence." I chucked and said "I think that's already taken!" A few days later, I asked again and received the same response. He advised me to google the words, and when I did, I sat back in my chair and smiled. The definition of "declaration" is "affirmation" and "independence" is "freedom." How perfect is that!

Crystals and stones hold vibrations; they can effectively help us with healing on every level. The amethyst crystal holds the vibrational essence of the violet flame and will heighten your decreeing. Some of the attributes are the following: amplifies energy, provides protection, cleanses negative energy, boosts spiritual awareness, opens psychic abilities, provides inner peace, heightens meditation, brings balance to life, relieves stress, aids in communication. Another powerful stone is the Super 7, also known as Melody's Stone. It's a naturally formed combination of amethyst and six other stones. There's a dynamic decree from the Super 7 crystal in the decree section.

How to create the life of your dreams with the Violet Flame?

Now that you understand the transmuting power of the violet flame and how it works, you can successfully bring it into your life to help create all you desire. When I first heard, *I'm responsible for my life/reality*, I thought, *How can that be? I'm just a spoke on the big wheel of life. How can I be in control?* As my understanding grew of the Law of Attraction, and I began to grasp that everything that happened to me I attracted, I realized I wasn't a spoke on a wheel, or even the wheel, I was the driver of the car. This realization changed my life forever!

The Law of Attraction is a universal law. It's science, plain and simple—sound familiar? When you have a thought or feeling, you emanate a vibration, which attracts like vibrations. Every thought or feeling you have has a vibrational signature you're sending out into the Universe. If you want a relationship, fulfilling job, prosperity, happiness, peace, etc., you must be in vibrational harmony with it for it to manifest into your reality. Your words, thoughts and feelings must match what you desire. In order to attract happiness, you need to find a thought—any good-feeling thought—or feeling to put you in that vibration. It's your vibration that brings about your desire—not your words, but the words help you get to that vibrational frequency. Hence, the violet flame has the ability to do just that, with minimal effort.

Every second of the day your thought forms radiate out to the Universe, bringing back a vibrational match. When you feel fear, you'll attract fear. When you feel happy, happy people and events will cross your path. You're emitting a signal like a radio station. It's critical to become aware of your thoughts and intentions by observing—without judgment—the monkey mind chatter. If you wish to change your life, you must first change within. As you claim your power and become aware and conscious of your thoughts in the present NOW moment, you'll become a deliberate creator of your life. In all situations, ask yourself, *What do I wish to create in this moment?* Then imagine what you desire. And don't forget to add in the colorful details.

When a diminishing thought surfaces, invoke the violet flame to transmute that thought pattern or belief with a decree. A contradiction may be unworthiness, fear, lack of confidence, the dreaded . . . what ifs. Or possibly when an emotion of fear or anger crops up—invoke the violet flame. If you're feeling tension or stress—flame it! If you set your intention in the morning and during your day you become aware of a thought which is contradictory, invoke the violet flame. Maybe you've set your intention for an attractive, fulfilling, meaningful job, and then you have an unfavorable thought, like *I'm not worthy*, or *This will never happen*, or *I don't deserve to be happy*. At that instant, the violet flame is vitally important. It's the opportune moment to transmute those disempowering thoughts and restate your intention. Maintain positivity, see/live the end result, have fun daydreaming while feeling exuberant, and then surrender.

Or suppose you intend to manifest abundance, and for no apparent reason have a feeling of lack. That's the perfect opportunity to invoke the violet flame to transmute the associated fear from your emotional body. Fear and buried unconscious beliefs are hidden until a situation triggers them and brings them to the surface to be permanently transmuted, so they can no longer keep you a prisoner. You're an energy alchemist, and the violet flame will set you free. As humanity is awakening and shifting to higher consciousness, this is an important time to shut the door on the negatives of the past and transmute miscreations. By releasing thought patterns, buried beliefs—and shining the Light on them—you can transform anything in your life. Determine which people and things are not serving your highest good, feeding your soul or providing a quality of life. As these attachments are transmuted by the violet flame, your vibration will rise, flooding your life with peace, well-being, happiness and all that you desire.

Think of the Universe as a waiter in a restaurant, taking your order. When you place your order, you don't go into fear and storm into the kitchen if your food doesn't come right away. You have faith and know, it will. The Universe knows the perfect timing for your desires to manifest and will rearrange itself to accommodate you. I've witnessed this many times, almost like a magician doing a card trick or making something disappear and reappear as something else. As I use the violet flame to maintain a high vibrational frequency, magical things happen. It's uncanny. One such time I received a call from my very competent accountant, informing me I owed a significant amount of taxes. I did my best to diminish the fear welling up and began invoking the violet flame. Two weeks later his office notified me my taxes were ready to be picked up; I owed X dollars—an amount dramatically lower. I sat back in disbelief. When I stopped by the office, I asked what happened. But it was as if there was no recollection of the earlier conversation.

When obstacles occurs, invoking the violet flame will do wonders. All healing is a process—grief, illness, sorrow—and the flame will have you feeling like yourself in no time. When we experience tragedy, it can become stuck in our energy body—hard to break free of. Other times we hold on to hardship, letting it become part of our persona. The longer this stays in our energy field, the less we notice, and then it becomes ingrained as our self.

There are seven Violet Star Angels assigned to anyone who actively decrees. Their mission is to help you navigate your journey with grace, ease and fun. You may call on them to help with any issue. To summon their assistance, there are two decrees included in this book. Talk to them as you would an old friend. They are eager and willing to help.

Violet Flame Decrees . . .

Violet Flame, burst forth relief
& transmute limiting beliefs
Violet Flame, blaze through my impediments
& bring mighty miraculous benefits
Violet Flame, obliterate all obstructions
& illuminate a crystal path of instructions
Violet Flame, revive my soul
& bestow me with being whole

∞∞∞

Violet Flame, Violet Flame,
transmute the mire
Violet Flame, Violet Flame,
transmute ill will and desire
Violet Flame, Violet Flame,
transmute false self and illusion
Violet Flame, Violet Flame,
transmute detritus and delusion

I AM the Violet Flame

Remembering the power contained

Calling upon thee to transmute the pain

Heightening my connection without constrain

Revealing my purpose with joy and anticipation

Recalling my magnificence as a being of Light

Reviewing the past with a grateful heart

Acknowledging St. Germain,

who lovingly remarks . . .

Use the Violet Flame without doubt

To transmute the detritus all about

Call forth its name, dance, sing and shout

Don't be ashamed to live in your light

Let your true self shine and sizzle bright

Like a beacon on a dark and starry night

Navigating others to find their inner might

You are vitally needed now to be the spark

Creating a new world where peace makes its mark.

I AM the Violet Flame, freedom is my game

I AM the Violet Flame, forgiveness always reigns

I AM the Violet Flame, transmuting stress and strain

I AM the Violet Flame, embracing all in Thy name

∞ ∞ ∞

Violet Flame, enfold me in forgiveness
of self and others
Transmuting the memories that binds and colors
Birthing forth feelings of compassion and grace
Remembering that love is the answer in every case

Violet Flame, engulf me in your radiance
Violet Flame, eradicate the decadence
Violet Flame, enable me to savor my experiences
Violet Flame, empower me to emerge victorious

∞∞∞

I AM invoking the Violet Flame
to harness its power
I AM chanting the Violet Flame
to ignite its fiery passion
I AM dancing the Violet Flame
to flow through my day
I AM decreeing the Violet Flame
to wash negativity away
I AM singing the Violet Flame
to harmonize my aura
I AM embracing the Violet Flame
to illuminate my way

I AM invoking the Violet Flame
to alleviate anguish
I AM invoking the Violet Flame
to rescind resentment
I AM invoking the Violet Flame
to resolve unforgiveness
I AM invoking the Violet Flame
to dissolve dissatisfaction
I AM invoking the Violet Flame
to shut the door on the past
I AM invoking the Violet Flame
to free the prisoner in me
I AM invoking the Violet Flame
to cut all ties that bind
Enfolding me with self-love and acceptance
Enabling me to experience life's abundance
Embracing enthusiasm, gratitude
and transcendence

I AM the pulse of the Violet Flame
flowing through my veins
I AM the beat of the Violet Flame
drumming in my heart
I AM the glimmer of the Violet Flame
twinkling in my eyes
I AM the buzzing of the Violet Flame
vibrating in my ears
I AM the throbbing of the Violet Flame
opening my crown
I AM the spark of the Violet Flame
igniting my passions
I AM the glow of the Violet Flame
radiating my beauty
I AM the flicker of the Violet Flame
titillating my senses
I AM the flare of the Violet Flame
inspiring my gifts
I AM the ashes of the Violet Flame
returning me to Source

Violet Flame, mend the wounds

Violet Flame, extract the pain

Violet Flame, unchain all burdens

Violet Flame, balance the karma

Violet Flame, extinguish my fears

Violet Flame, alter my afflictions

Violet Flame, singe my sorrows

Violet Flame, incinerate the anger

Violet Flame, char the grief

Violet Flame, transform my being

∞∞∞

Violet Flame, ignite the grace of God

Violet Flame, impart higher consciousness

Violet Flame, entrust me with your power

Violet Flame, expand my compassionate heart

Violet Flame, embellish me with joy and gratitude

Welcoming Oneness among the Kingdoms on Earth

I AM the Violet Flame blazing through my veins
infusing my blood with life force flow
I AM the Violet Flame blazing through my feet
carrying me on my journey, without defeat
I AM the Violet Flame blazing through my bones
strengthening my alignment in harmonious tones
I AM the Violet Flame blazing through my eyes
discerning what's mine to do
bringing my talents into view
I AM the Violet Flame blazing through my ears
hearing the angels' whispers loud and clear
I AM the Violet Flame blazing through my heart
beating with my true spirit and loving thoughts
I AM the Violet Flame blazing through my hands
bestowing healing to me and all I can
I AM the Violet Flame blazing through my mind
transmuting miscreations into the
Light of the Divine

I AM the mighty Violet Flame
I AM the invincible Violet Flame
I AM the unstoppable Violet Flame
I AM calling forth its spiritual power
to cleanse my chakras, each and every hour
to align the spin, the sheen, the shimmer
to balance, enhance and discover
Revitalizing my root chakra, to trust all is well
Scintillating my sacral, to embody pure pleasure
Illuminating my solar plexus, to confidently create
Opening my heart, to compassionately love
Strengthening my throat, to speak only truth
Clearing my Third Eye, to intuitively imagine
Expanding my crown, to embrace who I AM

Violet Flame, calling forth your worth
To bring about a resounding rebirth
For this great country and beyond
Restoring freedom to me and all mankind

∞∞∞

Violet Flame, incinerate the dirt and grime
Transmuting from this and all lifetimes
Anything less than the Will of the Divine
Vibrating the electrons faster all the time

∞∞∞

Violet Flame, you are a spiritual fire
Igniting my passions and desires
Bursting my unique gifts like a bonfire
Rejoicing and hearing an angel choir

Violet Flame, you are the Freedom Flame
Call forth its name to transmute away
Violet Flame, you are God's greatest gift
Call forth its name to enlighten and lift
Violet Flame, you are Divine alchemy
Call forth its name to cleanse magically
Violet Flame, you are from Heaven above
Bestowing us in God's Power and Love

∞∞∞

Violet Flame, ignite the connection
By amplifying ethereal communication
With guides, higher self and the Mighty One
Awakening the soul's blueprint within the
Great Central Sun

Violet Flame, transmute the anger,
the pain, the sorrow
Violet Flame, transmute the grief and
emptiness from tomorrow
Violet Flame, heal the despair in my heart
from the death of my loved one's recent depart
To know I was forgiven of all past transgressions
Helps me find peace with the memories
and recollections
Gift me to understand the grace of compassion
Fully filling the void with God's love & satisfaction

I AM invoking the Violet Flame
Calling forth full power in its name
To disperse all issues with control and fear
Freeing me to live in peace and good cheer
Fulling trusting the Divine has a plan in place
Guiding my adventure with ease and grace
Going with the flow and having a ball
Surrendering to the best outcome for all
Letting intuitive guidance be my oar
With faith in place my journey will soar

∞∞∞

Violet Flame, you rock my world
Violet Flame, you are so cool
Violet Flame, you cleanse the grime
Violet Flame, you make me shine
Violet Flame you keep me aligned
Violet Flame, you are so fine
Violet Flame, you are better than wine
Violet Flame, you are Divine

I AM the Violet Flame defragging my consciousness
of anything less than God's opulence
I AM the Violet Flame deleting from my mind
outdated programs not aligned
I AM the Violet Flame clearing all jams
bestowing self-love and focus to my path
I AM the Violet Flame installing new programs
birthing self-mastery and determination
I AM the Violet Flame updating my awareness
with alacrity, passion and mindfulness
Receiving the guidance and grace from God
each and every day without delay

Violet Flame transforms the mighty crystals,
guarding Mother Earth
Violet Flame transforms the mighty crystals,
assisting with rebirth
Violet Flame transforms the mighty crystals,
cleansing day and night
Violet Flame transforms the mighty crystals,
amplifying the Light
Violet Flame transforms the mighty crystals,
vibrating with a sound
Violet Flame transforms the mighty crystals,
radiating to all mankind
Violet Flame transforms the mighty crystals,
purging like a shower
Violet Flame transforms the mighty crystals,
restoring to full power
Violet Flame transforms the mighty crystals,
gifting a glorious ascension
Violet Flame transforms the mighty crystals,
awakening all to a higher dimension

I AM calling forth the Violet Flame
To transmute each and every hour
Anything less than God's perfect plan
Fulfilling my mission and soul's purpose
By expressing my gifts in the world of form
Benefiting and awakening all mankind
With the wisdom and knowledge
of the Mighty Ones
Aiding with ascension and astute awareness
Bringing freedom and lightness to everyone
Allowing our spirits to fly as we become One

Violet Flame empower me to be
The best and most awesome aspect of me
Allow me to remember my true soul's light
Guide me to encompass my Divine birthright

I AM invoking the Violet Flame
cleansing *all* political systems of abuse
I AM invoking the Violet Flame
removing from those involved *all* greed and misuse
I AM invoking the Violet Flame
transmuting from *all* leaders
anything less than integrity
I AM invoking the Violet Flame
restoring *all* world financial
systems with prosperity
I AM invoking God's Golden Light
to fill *all* voids created
Liberating *all* to live, thrive and flourish
with victorious elation
Eradicating poverty consciousness
from *all* mankind
Bestowing freedom for *all* and
a government by the I AM

Violet Flame,
transmute magically
from humanity
my family
with gravity & sanctity
bestowing lavishly & expansively
restoring vitality & sanity
bringing veracity
in totality
living enthusiastically
in this fantasy

I AM invoking the Violet Flame
to excoriate the anger
I AM invoking the Violet Flame
to incinerate the irritation
I AM invoking the Violet Flame
to get to the root of the matter
Freeing me to embrace happiness and positivity
Bestowing joviality, well-being and salvation
Empowering my uniqueness to radiate brilliantly

I AM invoking the Violet Flame
to disperse delusions
from my DNA and ancestry
I AM invoking the Violet Flame
to dispel dread
from my DNA and ancestry
I AM invoking the Violet Flame
to diffuse doubt
from my DNA and ancestry
I AM invoking the Violet Flame
to dissolve discomfort
from my DNA and ancestry
I AM invoking the Violet Flame
to dissipate destitution
from my DNA and ancestry
Availing my heart to abounding abundance
Activating my crystalline solar light body
without reluctance

I AM the Violet Flame vibrationally aligning
my etheric body
I AM the Violet Flame vibrationally aligning
my mental body
I AM the Violet Flame vibrationally aligning
my emotional body
I AM the Violet Flame vibrationally aligning
my Higher Self
I AM the Violet Flame vibrationally aligning
my I AM Presence
I AM the Violet Flame vibrationally aligning
with my true essence

I AM invoking the Violet Flame
To transmute excess body weight in a healthy way
Restoring my being to its ideal body weight
Bringing harmony and balance to every cells state

I AM invoking the Violet Flame
to transform my lower self through and through
bringing my Higher Self into view
I AM invoking the Violet Flame
to transmute fear, fret and blame
empowering my Higher Self to regain the reins
I AM invoking the Violet Flame
to eliminate all struggle and strife
freeing my Higher Self to mentor me through life
I AM invoking the Violet Flame
to diminish discord and pain from thee
allowing my light to envision my true identity

I AM the Violet Flame . . .

God's blue flame of Power

I AM the Violet Flame . . .

God's pink flame of Love

I AM the Violet Flame merging as one

I AM the Violet Flame enveloping my heart

I AM the Violet Flame

remembering my magnificence

I AM the Violet Flame eternally appreciative

∞∞∞

Violet Flame, transmute from thee

all that is hindering my awakening

Violet Flame, transform from thee

all lower self-tendencies imbedded in me

Violet Flame, burn from thee

all restrictions impeding me to be carefree

Violet Flame, incinerate from thee

all less than my Divine Blueprint

to the highest degree

I AM invoking the Violet Flame
to transmute poverty consciousness
I AM invoking the Violet Flame
to transmute anything less than opulence
I AM invoking the Violet Flame
to transmute and burn all impediments away
Freeing me to blossom and prosper
Embracing an abundant life from my Father

∞∞∞

Violet Flame, free all mankind
from the chains and burdens of the mind
Violet Flame, cleanse the land
from all remnants of war fought by man
Violet Flame, eradicate the memories
from all involved in the treacheries
Violet Flame, revive comity
between all countries and humanity

I AM invoking the golden orb of Violet Flame
Relinquishing all misuse in Thy Name
Gracing all mankind as we make a fresh start
Beating it forth from my heart
Pulsing through the Sacred Heart of Mother Earth
Surging through the layers, cleansing her girth
Eradicating with high voltage to purge the land
Bringing peace, brotherhood and
Oneness as we band

∞∞∞

I AM a golden sun of Violet Flame
claiming victory in God's name
I AM a golden sun of Violet Flame
transmuting negativity, anger and blame
I AM a golden sun of Violet Flame
transforming miscreations, eradicating shame
I AM a golden sun of Violet Flame
healing my body, rejuvenating the same
I AM a golden sun of Violet Flame
Bestowing peace and prosperity, I proclaim

I AM the Violet Flame
illuminating my mind
I AM the Violet Flame
expanding my heart
I AM the Violet Flame
filling me with grace
I AM the Violet Flame
protecting me and my space
I AM the Violet Flame
eradicating dirt and grime
I AM the Violet Flame
transmuting all the time
I AM the Violet Flame
restoring harmony and balance
I AM the Violet Flame
discovering my talents

I AM grateful for the Violet Flame
giving praise and rejoice in its name
I AM grateful for the Violet Flame
cleansing my aura and balancing the same
I AM grateful for the Violet Flame
lifting me higher on this plane
I AM grateful for the Violet Flame
returning my awareness to whence I came
I AM grateful for the Violet Flame
igniting its power to grace the Milky Way

I AM breathing the Violet Flame,
revitalizing my being
I AM ingesting the Violet Flame,
nourishing my body
I AM summoning the Violet Flame,
saturating my aura
I AM singing the Violet Flame,
uplifting my vibration
I AM toning the Violet Flame,
transmuting the unwanted
I AM dancing the Violet Flame,
creating magic
I AM sensing the Violet Flame,
discovering its potentiality
I AM the Violet Flame,
sparking change to this game

I AM invoking the Violet Flame
to purify the air
I AM invoking the Violet Flame
to rejuvenate the water
I AM invoking the Violet Flame
to restore the food
I AM invoking the Violet Flame
to purge the land
I AM invoking the Violet Flame
to cleanse the planet
I AM invoking the Violet Flame
to bring wholeness to Gaia
Freeing all life to thrive and flourish
Living on the New Earth
where well-being will rein

Violet Star Angel Decrees

Astralia, Migdalia, Theostralia, Newalia,
Deepalia, Verriglia, Rostaglia

Violet Star Angels, I beckon your fiery Light
to navigate me along the avenues of life
Freeing my inner child bringing
newness and delight
Allowing my spirit to soar to the highest of heights
Inspiring me to manifest each moment with glee
Creating my reality as the director of this dream
Taking control, command, and claiming my power
Over all that diminishes and makes me cower
Reminding me of the truth of why I AM here
Bringing my gifts to the world which I hold so dear

∞∞∞

Violet Star Angels, I call forth your might
Bringing freedom to me from my mind's
constant plight
Settling the clamor to a deafening void
Birthing crystal clear guidance dispersing the noise
Intuitively harnessing my inner self's wisdom
Allowing me to flow with my soul's song rhythm
Providing peace from the chatter that once
was non-stop
Freeing me to live, create, soar and shout

Super 7 Crystal Message

We, the Super Seven crystals,
come to give you a boost
Sparking your spirit and reminding
you of your truth
When you gather in groups larger than one
we multiply your intentions
far greater than the sum
We hold the knowledge of your soul's course
Relentlessly guiding your awakening
to become one with Source
By transmuting old ways and
blossoming new growth
You'll embrace your brilliance
and emerge the most
We'll push your soul till surrender begins
and full awareness discovers the treasure
that's buried within

One-Liners

I AM invoking the Violet Flame to transmute anything less than God's Will from my physical body, energy field, chakras and meridians.

I AM invoking the Violet Flame to transmute this (thought) and similar thoughts.

I AM invoking the Violet Flame to transmute anything less than God's Will from my physical body, restoring every cell to vibrant health and physical vitality.

I AM invoking the Violet Flame to transmute all limiting behaviors not in alignment with my highest good and that of God's Will.

I AM invoking the Violet Flame to transmute anything less than God's Will from this _____ (food, water, space, home, office, building, land, planet, etc.).

I AM invoking the Violet Flame to cleanse and balance my chakras.

I AM placing a cosmic filter of Violet Light between me and the television, computer, and phone to transmute all discordant energy.

I AM invoking the Violet Flame to cleanse all cords that exist between me and (person's name).

I AM invoking the Violet Flame to transmute anything less than God's Will from all banking and financial systems bringing prosperity, abundance and freedom for all.

Create your own affirmations:

I AM invoking the Violet Flame to transmute . . .

Declaration of Independence

I AM a Violet Star

Guardian of the Flame

God's greatest gift

Purging the Earth

From eons of lifetimes

Ours and others

No need to blame

I AM a Violet Star

Bringing forth Higher Power

Defeating fear

Dispelling delusions

Breaking barriers

Holding heart consonance

LOVE is the answer

I AM a Violet Star

Collectively in Oneness

Accepting of others

With compassion and kindness

As our journeys unwind

Discovering the dream

That lies within

I AM a Violet Star

Contributing my gifts

To grace all mankind

That knows no bounds

To cleanse and restore

Like never before

Bestowing freedom & wholeness

I AM a Violet Star

Transmuting relentlessly

With my flaming wand

Healing humanity

Personally and collectively

Obtaining self-mastery

And higher consciousness

I AM a Violet Star

Shining brighter

Illuminating the way

Claiming my power

Ascending to new heights

With the Violet Flame

Manifesting Victory for ALL!

I AM a Violet Star . . .

a Son & Daughter of St. Germain

Violet Pictures

The violet light started showing up in pictures October 2013, when I was on a spiritual journey. Since then, its made itself known frequently . . . sometimes way too often. This picture of my cat, Sunny, was actually taken after 2013, even though the date shows 2005; the camera defaults to that date when no date is set. My camera is a Sony digital model, circa 2004. No enhancements were done. It looks exactly like this when viewed in the camera. Every time violet light occurs in a picture, I'm outside and it's always the same hue of violet.

This picture was taken during a golf tournament with a fellow teammate, as the violet light saturated us. The eBook shows these pictures in vibrant violet color. You may also find them at www.facebook.com/The-Violet-Flame-A-Game-Changer

Parting Words

Oh my Beloveds, I trust these decrees will serve you well, for they are time tested. Let this be the spark to ignite your transformation. The violet flame is a glorious gift to be savored and shared, to enlighten and lift. Do not delay in transmuting self-imposed limitations. As you embrace the violet flame great changes will abound. There's a bright beautiful world waiting for your light. There will come a time in the not too distant future, when all of humanity will realize its power, and it will become a part of daily life. So many incredible changes are occurring at warp speed, and you are part of this transformation. Relish the journey and flame away!

~ St. Germain

Acknowledgments

I wish to thank my editor extraordinaire, Margaret A. Harrell, who guided me during this sometimes arduous publishing process, while providing immense encouragement and eagerly sharing her extensive knowledge.

And enormous appreciation to my Violet Star sisters and brothers, who have graciously given me a loving platform to create, grow, evolve and share my gifts to help others.

And last but not least by any means, I wish to acknowledge St. Germain, who has generously guided me on my journey as a spiritual teacher, friend and trusted companion.

About the Author

Denise Kane is a spiritual teacher, channel and Reiki Master with a healing center, Butterfly Reiki, in Raleigh, NC. She's the founder of the Violet Stars Lightworkers Group, which conducts weekly gatherings, under St. Germain's direction, to raise personal and collective consciousness. During her thirty-eight year career with a major airline, she knew there had to be more to life than changing passenger's seat assignments and getting planes to depart on time. In 2006 she woke up, as the saying goes, which opened up the world of angels and changed her views. Her studies feverishly continued as she added to her healer's tool belt with a variety of modalities and angel initiations. Denise had been a corporate executive, working for the airlines; now, in a little more than a blink of an eye, she finds herself firmly on a totally different path, determined to play her role in bringing the violet flame to heal the world.

For news, updates, events and sharing, visit ...
www.facebook.com/The-Violet-Flame-A-Game-Changer

Check out Denise's YouTube channel for weekly messages and guided meditations from St. Germain.

Made in the USA
Middletown, DE
24 January 2020